EXPLORING INDIA'S ASTROLOGICAL REMEDIES

A JOURNEY THROUGH THE TRADITIONS AND PRACTICES OF INDIA'S ASTROLOGICAL REMEDIES

DR. JAGADEESH PILLAI

Made with ♥ on the Notion Press Platform
www.notionpress.com

|| Dedicated to all wisdom seekers around the world ||

Contents

Contents

ABOUT THE AUTHOR

Dr. Jagadeesh Pillai is a renowned Guinness World Record holder, writer, and researcher hailing from Varanasi, also known as the abode of Lord Shiva. With a Ph.D. in Vedic Science and a range of creative ideas and achievements, he is a true polymath. He is the author of more than 100 books including Research Publications. Although his roots can be traced back to Kerala, the people of Varanasi hold him in high regard and affectionately consider him one of their own.

Dr. Pillai has achieved four Guinness World Records in the following subjects:

"Script to Screen" - In this record, Dr. Pillai produced and directed an animation film within the shortest time possible, breaking the previous record set by Canadians. He has also received numerous national and international awards and recognitions for this achievement.

Longest Line of Postcards - For this record, Dr. Pillai created a line of 16,300 postcards on the occasion of the 163rd anniversary of Indian Postal Day. The event also included a questionnaire about the Indian flag.

Largest Poster Awareness Campaign - Dr. Pillai designed an awareness campaign on the subject of "Beti Bachao - Beti Padhao" (Save the Girl Child - Educate the Girl Child) to achieve this record.

Largest Envelope - In tribute to the Indian Prime Minister's

"Make in India" initiative, Dr. Pillai created a 4000 square meter envelope using waste paper to achieve this record.

Attempted - **70000 Candles on a 210 kg Cake** - To celebrate the 70th Indian Independence Day, Dr. Pillai attempted to light 70,000 candles on a 210 kg cake, which was recorded in World Records India.

Attempted - **Documentary on Dhamek Stupa of Sarnath in 17 Languages** - Dr. Pillai attempted to create a documentary on the Dhamek Stupa of Sarnath, dubbing it in 17 different languages. The result of this attempt is currently awaiting confirmation from the Guinness World Records.

Dr. Pillai is skilled in teaching the Bhagavad Gita, a Hindu scripture, and is popular among young people. He has helped many young people improve their lives through his motivational teachings.

In addition to teaching, he has composed and sung numerous Sanskrit Bhajans and patriotic songs.

He has also written and directed several short films and documentaries for awareness campaigns, and has volunteered with the police in both UP and Kerala to spread awareness about various issues through videos and photography.

Incredibly, he has produced and directed over 100 documentaries about the city of Varanasi, all on his own.

He has also helped and guided more than 25 boys and girls to achieve world records through creative and innovative methods. He is a multifaceted person who uses his intellect and the blessings given to him by God to excel in various areas. He is both a teacher and a student, always learning and teaching, and is able to master any subject he comes across.

He is a selfless social activist and motivational speaker who has overcome struggles and failures to become a successful and enthusiastic individual with a rich life experience.

In addition to his work with the Bhagavad Gita, he is also an efficient Tarot card reader, Astro-Vastu consultant, and a talented singer and composer. He has sung the entire Ram Charita Manas and Bhagavad Gita in his own compositions, and has sung the phrase "Lokah Samastha Sukhino Bhavantu" in 50 different languages. He is currently working on a detailed and scientific study of Vedas, Upanishads, Puranas, and the Bhagavad Gita. He has also composed and sung the Hanuman Chalisa and Gayatri Mantra in 108 and 1008 different compositions, respectively.

Awards - Four Times Guinness World Records, Winner of Mahatma Gandhi Vishwa Shanti Puraskar, Mahatma Gandhi Global Peace Ambassador, Kashi Ratna Award, Dr. APJ Abdul Kalam Motivational Person of the Year 2017, Mother Teresa Award, Indira Gandhi Priyadarshini Award, Bharat Vikas Ratna Award, Udyog Ratna Award, Vigyan Prasar Award, Poorvanchal Ratn Samman.

PREFACE

India is renowned for its rich and vibrant astrological traditions. This book, The Indian Astrological Remedies: An Exploration of Indian astrological remedies and practices, seeks to explore the culture, art, and tradition behind Indian astrology and its various remedies.

This book is intended to serve as an introduction to the rich history and culture of Indian astrological remedies for readers who are new to the subject. It explores astrology and karma, the significance of gemstones, Vedic remedies for health, Vedic astrology for career and job, astrology remedies for marriage, Vedic remedies for betterment in love life, the power of mantra chanting, Rudra Abhishek for health, donation and its importance, and the future of Indian astrological remedies.

The book draws on research from a variety of sources, including interviews with key figures in the Indian astrological community, archival materials, and cultural analysis. I have also conducted extensive field research in India, including attending festivals, interviewing astrologers, and visiting locations associated with the production of astrological remedies. Through this research, I hope to provide readers with a comprehensive understanding of the Indian astrological industry and its various components.

I am deeply passionate about the art of Indian astrology and hope that this book will help to spread the appreciation of this wonderful form of cultural expression. I believe that

Indian astrology has a great deal to offer to the world and I am excited to share its cultural and historical significance with my readers.

I

Introduction to Indian Astrological Remedies

Indian Astrology is an ancient system of knowledge, rooted in the Vedas, which is based on the belief that the stars, planets, and other celestial bodies have an influence on the lives of humans on Earth. Astrology in India, or Jyotish as it is known in Sanskrit, is an integral part of Indian culture and heritage. Astrological remedies are a key component of Vedic astrology, and are used to help in overcoming life's difficulties, resolving issues and gaining success in various areas of life.

Astrological remedies are based on the idea that the planets, stars and other celestial bodies are the cause of both positive and negative influences in life. Astrology can be used to identify and understand the influences, and to then create remedies to counter them. The remedies are often prescribed in the form of rituals, chanting of mantras, donations to charities, or specific changes in lifestyle and behaviour.

The main focus of astrological remedies is to reduce the ill-effects of negative influences, while also helping to strengthen positive influences. The remedies are based on the belief that by making the necessary changes, one can overcome the difficulties caused by bad planetary influences. The remedies are also believed to help enhance the effects of good influences, leading to better luck and success in life.

There are many different types of remedies used in Indian astrology. These include gemstone therapy, pooja, homam, and yantras, among many others. Gemstone therapy is the use of gemstones to counter the bad effects of certain planets, while pooja and homam are rituals performed to appease the gods and gain their blessings. Yantras are sacred diagrams that are used to help focus energy and bring about positive change.

In addition to these remedies, there are also various other forms of astrological remedies such as yagya, yagna, mantra chanting, and donations. Yagya is a ritual in which offerings are made to the gods and divine beings in order to gain their blessings. Yagna is a process of sacrifice and prayer which is used to appease the gods and invoke their blessings. Mantra chanting is the recitation of sacred mantras to gain spiritual enlightenment and power. Donations are made to charities or temples to gain the blessings of the gods.

"Vedic wisdom is the light that guides us on our journey through life."

ᘓ

II

Astrology and Karma

Astrology and karma are two of the most powerful forces in Indian spiritual practice. They are both deeply intertwined, and each has its own unique set of dynamics and influences. Astrology is the study of the movements and positions of the planets, stars, and other celestial bodies, and how these movements and positions can affect our lives. Karma is the spiritual law of cause and effect and the idea that our actions have consequences both in this life and in future lives.

Karma is a central belief in Hinduism and Buddhism, and astrology is used to understand and interpret the effects of karma in our lives. Astrologers use the positions of the planets and the movements of the stars to predict the outcomes of our actions and the effects of karma on individuals. According to astrologers, the planets and stars influence our lives in various ways, and the influence of karma is felt through the movements of the planets.

In addition to understanding the effects of karma, astrology can also be used to make predictions about our future and our destiny. Astrologers use the positions of the planets and stars to make predictions about our future, and these predictions can be used to plan our lives and make decisions. Astrology can also help us understand our past, as the positions of the planets can provide insight into past events and experiences that have shaped our lives.

Karma and astrology are closely related, and their influence on our lives can be seen in many aspects. Astrology can help us to understand the effects of our actions and the influence of karma in our lives, while karma can help us to understand the consequences of our actions. Together, they provide us with a better understanding of our lives and the spiritual forces that affect us. Astrology and karma can be used together to help us make wise decisions, plan our future, and gain insight into our past.

"Astrology is the study of the stars, but it is also the study of ourselves."

ꕥ

III

The Significance of Gemstones

Gemstones, also known as birthstones, have been used in Indian astrology for centuries as a way to bring good luck and positive energy into one's life. Each gemstone is associated with a specific planet, and when worn as a ring or pendant, it is believed to have a powerful influence on the wearer's life.

Indian astrology assigns specific gemstones to different planets based on the gemstone's color and chemical composition. For example, ruby is associated with the planet Sun, as it is a red gemstone, which is the color of the Sun. On the other hand, blue sapphire is associated with the planet Saturn, as it is a blue gemstone, which is the color of the Saturn.

Wearing the appropriate gemstone is believed to bring good luck and positive energy to the wearer. It is believed that the gemstone will strengthen the weak planet and neutralize the negative influence of malefic planets in the individual's horoscope. In addition, it is believed that the gemstone will help to bring prosperity, success, and happiness in one's life.

Gemstone therapy is considered a powerful tool for healing and self-improvement in Indian astrology. It is believed that wearing a gemstone can help to balance the energy of the body and mind, and can also help to remove negative energy and blockages.

It is important to note that not all gemstones are suitable for everyone. The choice of gemstone should be based on the individual's horoscope, as well as their personal preferences and budget. An astrologer or a gemologist can help to determine the best gemstone for an individual.

In conclusion, gemstones play a significant role in Indian astrology, as they are believed to bring good luck, positive energy and prosperity to the wearer. The choice of gemstone should be based on the individual's horoscope and personal preferences, and should be worn after consulting with a qualified astrologer or gemologist. By wearing the appropriate gemstone, one can improve their life and overcome any obstacles that may be holding them back.

"The wisdom of the Vedas is the wisdom of the ages, passed down through generations."

ᘓᘏ

IV

Vedic Remedies for Health

In ancient India, the Vedic tradition was not only a spiritual practice but also a holistic system of health and wellness. The Vedic texts contain a wealth of information on various remedies for various health conditions, including physical, mental, and emotional. These remedies are based on the belief that the human body is interconnected with the cosmos and that health can be attained by restoring balance and harmony within the body and with the environment.

One of the most important aspects of Vedic health is the concept of Ayurveda, which is a system of medicine that aims to prevent and treat illness by restoring balance to the body's three doshas or energies, Vata, Pitta, and Kapha. Ayurvedic remedies include the use of herbal medicines, massages, and dietary adjustments to balance the doshas and promote overall health.

Another important aspect of Vedic health is the practice of Yoga. Yoga is not only a physical practice but also a spiritual and mental one. It aims to unite the body, mind, and spirit and is believed to help reduce stress, improve flexibility, and promote overall well-being. Yoga practices such as asanas, pranayama, and meditation are believed to have a positive effect on various health conditions such as stress, anxiety, and depression.

Panchakarma is another important aspect of Vedic health. Panchakarma is a therapeutic cleansing process that aims to remove toxins from the body and restore balance to the doshas. The process involves a combination of therapies such as massage, steam therapy, and herbal enemas. Panchakarma is believed to help improve digestion, boost immunity, and promote overall well-being.

Vedic astrology is also an important aspect of Vedic health. Vedic astrology, also known as Jyotish, is a system of astrology originating in ancient India. It is considered an important aspect of Vedic health because it is believed to provide insight into an individual's physical, mental, and spiritual well-being. The positions of the planets and stars at the time of a person's birth are believed to influence their health, as well as their overall life path. Practitioners of Vedic astrology use this information to make recommendations for diet, exercise, and other lifestyle changes to promote overall health and well-being. Additionally, astrological remedies such as gemstones, mantras, and yantras are used to improve physical and mental health. It is also used to predict the timing of health issues and to recommend the best time for health-related treatments.

"Vedic astrology is the key to understanding our past, present, and future."

ꕤ

V

Vedic Astrology for Career and Job

In Vedic astrology, the positions of the planets and stars at the time of a person's birth are believed to influence their career and job prospects. The 10th house in a person's birth chart, which represents career and profession, is considered to be one of the most important factors in determining a person's career path. The planet in the 10th house, as well as the planets aspecting it, can provide insight into a person's natural abilities, interests, and potential career paths.

Additionally, the planets in the 2nd, 6th and 11th houses, which represent wealth, work, and income, can also provide insight into a person's earning potential and job prospects. For example, a strong Jupiter in the 2nd house can indicate success in business and finance, while a strong Mercury in the 6th house can indicate success in fields related to communication and technology.

Vedic astrology can also be used to predict the timing of job opportunities, promotions, and other career milestones. It is also used to recommend the best time for job interviews, business ventures, and other career-related decisions.

It's worth mentioning that Vedic Astrology is just one of many tools that can be used to gain insight into one's career path, and it should not be the only factor considered when making career decisions. It's always best to consult with a professional astrologer for personalized and accurate advice.

"Vedic wisdom teaches us to live in harmony with nature and the universe."

ജ

VI

Astrology Remedies for Marriage

In Vedic astrology, there are several astrological remedies that can be used to improve the prospects for marriage. These remedies can be used to alleviate negative influences on the 7th house of the birth chart, which represents marriage and partnerships.

Some common astrological remedies for marriage include:

Wearing a specific gemstone: Different gemstones are associated with different planets, and wearing the appropriate gemstone can strengthen the planet and improve the prospects for marriage.

Reciting mantras: Certain mantras are associated with specific planets, and reciting these mantras can help to improve the influence of that planet on the 7th house.

Performing poojas and yagnas: Performing certain poojas and yagnas can help to improve the overall balance of the birth chart and alleviate negative influences on the 7th house.

Donation: Donating to certain causes can help to alleviate malefic planetary influences on the 7th house and improve the prospects for marriage.

Fasting: Certain fasting days are associated with specific planets, and fasting on those days can help to improve the influence of that planet on the 7th house.

It's worth noting that some of these remedies may not be effective if the problem is not astrologically based, or if the problem is not related to the 7th house. It's always best to consult with a professional astrologer for personalized and accurate advice.

It's important to keep in mind that astrological remedies are supplementary and are not a substitute for efforts to improve one's personal and social interactions.

In addition to the astrological remedies mentioned above, there are also other remedies that can be used to improve the prospects for marriage. Some of these remedies include:

Performing the "Navgraha Shanti" Puja: The "Navgraha Shanti" Puja is a ritual that is performed to appease the nine planets and align them in your favor, this puja can help to improve the overall balance of the birth chart and alleviate negative influences on the 7th house.

Offerings to Lord Ganesha and Lord Vishnu: Offerings to Lord Ganesha and Lord Vishnu are believed to help remove obstacles and bring good luck in finding a suitable partner.

Wearing a Rudraksha: Wearing a Rudraksha is believed to help improve the overall balance of the birth chart and alleviate negative influences on the 7th house.

Consulting with an astrologer to analyze Dasha and Transits: Dasha and Transits are astrological cycles that can indicate the timing of major events, including marriage. An astrologer can analyze your Dasha and Transits to determine the best time to get married.

It's important to keep in mind that astrological remedies are supplementary and are not a substitute for efforts to improve one's personal and social interactions. It's always best to consult with a professional astrologer for personalized and accurate advice.

It's important to note that astrological remedies are not a guarantee of success and should be used in conjunction with other efforts to improve one's personal and social interactions. In addition to the astrological remedies, it is also important to work on improving oneself, developing good communication and relationship skills, and being open to new opportunities. It's always best to consult with a professional astrologer for personalized and accurate advice, and keep in mind that astrology is just one tool that can be used to gain insight into one's life and future.

"Astrology is not just about predicting the future, it's about understanding our place in the world."

ꕥ

VII

Vedic Remedies for Betterment in Love Life

In Vedic astrology, there are several astrological remedies that can be used to improve the prospects for love and relationships. These remedies can be used to alleviate negative influences on the 5th house of the birth chart, which represents love and romance.

Some common astrological remedies for love and relationships include:

Wearing a specific gemstone: Different gemstones are associated with different planets, and wearing the appropriate gemstone can strengthen the planet and improve the prospects for love.

Reciting mantras: Certain mantras are associated with

specific planets, and reciting these mantras can help to improve the influence of that planet on the 5th house.

Performing poojas and yagnas: Performing certain poojas and yagnas can help to improve the overall balance of the birth chart and alleviate negative influences on the 5th house.

Donating to certain causes: Donating to certain causes can help to alleviate malefic planetary influences on the 5th house and improve the prospects for love.

Fasting: Certain fasting days are associated with specific planets, and fasting on those days can help to improve the influence of that planet on the 5th house.

Offering to Venus: Venus is the planet of love and beauty, offering to Venus can help to improve the prospects for love and relationship.

It's worth noting that some of these remedies may not be effective if the problem is not astrologically based, or if the problem is not related to the 5th house. It's always best to consult with a professional astrologer for personalized and accurate advice.

It's important to keep in mind that astrological remedies are supplementary and are not a substitute for efforts to improve one's personal and social interactions, communication and emotional intelligence.

"Vedic wisdom is the path to enlightenment and self-realization."

VIII

The Power of Mantra Chanting

Mantra chanting is an ancient practice in Vedic tradition that is believed to have powerful spiritual and physical benefits. A mantra is a word or phrase that is repeated, usually in a meditative state, to focus the mind and tap into its spiritual energy. The repetition of a mantra is believed to help the mind to quiet down and become more focused, which can lead to a deeper sense of inner peace and clarity.

The power of mantra chanting lies in the vibrations created by the sounds of the mantras. Each sound is believed to have a specific vibrational frequency that corresponds to a specific chakra or energy center in the body. When a mantra is repeated, it creates a vibration that resonates with the corresponding energy center, helping to open, balance, and align the energy in that area. This can lead to improved physical and emotional health.

Mantra chanting is also believed to have a positive effect on the mind and emotions. Repeating a mantra can help to reduce stress and anxiety, promote feelings of calm and well-being, and improve overall mental and emotional balance.

It's important to mention that Mantra chanting should be done under the guidance of a qualified and experienced teacher, as improper pronunciation or intonation can lead to inefficacy and even negative effects.

In summary, mantra chanting is a powerful practice in Vedic tradition that can have spiritual and physical benefits, it's known for its ability to quiet the mind and promote inner peace, balance the energy centers, and improve overall health.

"Astrology helps us to understand the workings of the universe and our place within it."

ꝏ

IX

Rudra Abhishek for Health

Rudra Abhishek is a Hindu ritual that involves the worship of Lord Shiva, also known as Rudra. The ritual involves the recitation of specific mantras, offerings of various items such as milk, honey, and fruits, and the pouring of these offerings over a lingam (a symbol of Lord Shiva).

It is believed that performing Rudra Abhishek can have a positive impact on one's health. Lord Shiva is considered the destroyer of diseases and the bestower of health, and it is believed that performing the ritual can invoke his blessings for good health. Additionally, the recitation of mantras during the ritual is believed to have a purifying effect on the mind and body, promoting overall well-being.

It's also believed that Rudra Abhishek can help to alleviate negative influences of certain planets on one's health as per Vedic astrology. It's believed that performing Rudra

Abhishek can help to pacify malefic planetary influences and improve the overall balance of the birth chart.

It's worth noting that Rudra Abhishek is a complex ritual that is typically performed by a qualified and experienced priest, and It's important to perform the ritual with proper guidance and in the right manner to achieve the desired results.

In summary, Rudra Abhishek is a Hindu ritual that involves the worship of Lord Shiva and is believed to have positive effects on one's health. It's believed to invoke blessings for good health, alleviate negative planetary influences, and promote overall well-being. It's important to perform the ritual with proper guidance and in the right manner to achieve the desired results.

"Vedic wisdom is the foundation of a fulfilling and meaningful life."

ꙮ

X

Donations, Dakshina and Charity and Its Importance

In Vedic tradition, making donations, giving dakshina (gift or offering to a spiritual teacher or temple), and performing charity is considered an important aspect of spiritual practice. It is believed that giving to others can help to purify the mind and promote inner peace and contentment.

Donations and charity are believed to have a positive impact on one's karma, which is the sum total of a person's actions and their effects on the present and future lives. By giving to others, it is believed that one can accumulate good karma and create positive energy that will benefit them in the future.

Dakshina, which is the offering or gift given to a spiritual teacher or temple, is considered particularly important in Vedic tradition. It is believed that giving dakshina to a spiritual teacher helps to create a connection with the divine and promote spiritual growth. Giving dakshina to a temple is also considered to be beneficial, as it helps to support the maintenance and upkeep of the temple, which in turn promotes the spiritual well-being of the community.

It is worth mentioning that these donations and charity should not be done for the sake of gaining something but for the intention of helping and spreading kindness in the society.

In summary, making donations, giving dakshina and performing charity are considered important aspects of spiritual practice in Vedic tradition. They are believed to have a positive impact on one's karma, purify the mind, and promote inner peace and contentment. Giving dakshina to a spiritual teacher or temple is particularly important, as it helps to create a connection with the divine and promote spiritual growth.

"Vedic wisdom is the light that guides us on our journey through life."

XI

The Future of Indian Astrological Remedies

The future of Indian astrological remedies is uncertain, as it is a highly debated topic. Some people believe that astrological remedies will continue to be an important aspect of Indian culture, as they have been for thousands of years. They argue that the principles of astrology are based on sound scientific principles and that the remedies have been effective in helping people improve their lives.

On the other hand, some argue that astrological remedies are not based on scientific evidence and that they have no proven benefits. They argue that astrology is a pseudoscience, and that relying on astrological remedies can be harmful, as it can lead people to neglect important issues and real-world solutions.

It's worth noting that the practice of astrology and remedies has been around for centuries and it's deeply rooted in the Indian culture, it's unlikely to disappear completely but it's also important to consider that many people nowadays are looking for scientific and evidence-based approaches, this is why it's important for astrologers to be able to provide evidence-based and data-driven readings and remedies for their clients.

It's also worth mentioning that the use of Astrological remedies should be done under the guidance of a qualified and experienced astrologer, it's not a substitute for seeking medical or psychological help when needed.

In summary, the future of Indian astrological remedies is uncertain. Some people believe that astrological remedies will continue to be an important aspect of Indian culture, while others argue that they are not based on scientific evidence and can be harmful. It's important for astrologers to be able to provide evidence-based and data-driven readings and remedies for their clients and to be used under the guidance of a qualified and experienced astrologer.

Other Books Of The Author

1. The Moments When I Met God
2. Kashiyile Theertha Pathangal
3. GURU GYAN VANI
4. Abhiprerak Gita
5. ASSI SE JAIN GHAT TAK
6. Hopelessness of Arjuna
7. The Soul and It's True Nature
8. Sense of Action (Karma)
9. Action through Wisdom
10. Action through Wisdom
11. THEORY AND PRACTICAL OF EVERY ACTION
12. LOGICAL UNDERSTANDING OF THE SUPREME
13. THE IMPERISHABLE SUPREME
14. Yatra Nishadraj se Hanuman Ghat Tak
15. Yatra Karnatak Ghat se Raja Ghat Tak
16. Yatra Pandey Ghat se Prayagraj Ghat Tak
17. Yatra Ranjendra Prasad Ghat se Dattatreya Ghat Tak
18. YaatraSindhiya Ghat se Gwaliar Ghat Tak
19. Yatra Mangala Gauri Ghat se Hanuman Gadhi Ghat Tak
20. Yatra Gaay Ghat Se Nishad Ghat Tak
21. MAA GANGA, GHATEN EVM UTSAV
22. Ganga Arti Dev Deepavali evam Any Utsav
23. Potentials of Digitalized India
24. VEDIC CONSCIOUSNESS
25. A Brief Introduction to Vedic Science
26. Kashi ke Barah Jyotirling
27. IMPACT OF MOTIVATION
28. Let's have a Milky Way Journey
29. Color Therapy in a Nutshell

30. Rigveda in a Nutshell
31. Yajurveda in a Nutshell
32. Samveda in a Nutshell
33. Atharva Veda in a Nutshell
34. Ayushman Bhava - Ayurveda
35. Srimad Bhagavad Gita and Upanishad Connection
36. Srimad Bhagavad Gita - an attempt to summarize each chapter.
37. Facts and Impact of Nakshatra
38. Astro Gems - NAVARATNA
39. Ekadashi - A Concise Overview
40. A Concise View of Hanuman Chalisa
41. Inspirational Gita
42. Nakshatraranyam
43. Summary of 18 Mahapuranas
44. Synopsis of 18 Upa Puranas
45. Rigvediya Upanishads
46. Shukla Yajurvediya Upanishads
47. Krishna Yajurvediya Upanishads
48. Samavediya Upanishads
49. Atharvavediya Upanishads
50. The Seven Great Sages
51. From Rocket Scientist to President Dr. APJ Abdul Kalam
52. The Visionary's Voice - Quotes of Dr. APJ Abdul Kalam
53. The Wisdom of Swami Vivekananda: Insights and Inspiration from a Legendary Spiritual Teacher
54. Ayurvedic Remedies from the Garden
55. Sages and Seers
56. Rising Strong – Motivational Stories of Women
57. Beyond Flames -Mystery stories of Funeral Ghat Manikarnika
58. The Origins of Tulsi: A Look at the Mythological Roots of the Plant"

59. The Holistic Cow: A Look at the Physical, Spiritual, and Cultural Importance of Cows in India
60. Arts of Healing
61. Exploring the Divine
62. Understanding Five Elements
63. The Etymology of Ram
64. Symbols of India
65. Voice of Change (About Speeches of Great Men)
66. She Speaks (About Speeches of Great Women)
67. Patriotism on Celluloid – Brief About Patriotic Films
68. The Music of Motivation: A Brief Guide to Inspirational Film Songs
69. Unlocking the Secrets of the Dashopanishads
70. A Cultural Mosaic
71. Ancient Traditions, Modern Minds
72. Ecos of Ancient Wisdom
73. Beneath the Surface
74. From Temples to Ashrams
75. Sages of the Subcontinent
76. The Art of Healling (Ayurveda, Yoga & Naturopathy)
77. Indian Kitchen
78. The Festivals of India
79. The Indian Epics Retold
80. The Power of Mantras
81. The Indian River Ganges
82. The Indian Architecture
83. Rites of Passage
84. The Indian Silk Road
85. The Indian Literature
86. The Indian Villages
87. The Indian Folks & Crafts
88. The Way of Buddha
89. The Ramayan of Tulsidas

90. Astrological Remedies
91. The Secret Power of Motivation
92. Secret of Developing your Inner Strength

CONTACT

DR. JAGADEESH PILLAI

PhD in Vedic Science

Four Times Guinness World Record Holder

Winner of Mahatma Gandhi Vishwa Shanti Puraskar and Global Peace Ambassador

Gemology, Astro & Vastu Consultant - Spiritual Counselor

Consultant for designing World Record Ideas

Efficient Tarot Card Reader

9839093003

myrichindia@gmail.com

drjagadeeshpillai@facebook

drjagadeeshpillai@instagram

jagadeeshpillai@youtube

www. JAGADEESHPILLAI.com

|| LOKAHA SAMASTHAHA SUKHINO BHAVANTU ||

9 798889 513865

Printed by Libri Plureos GmbH in Hamburg, Germany